mr.manners

ANNA POST

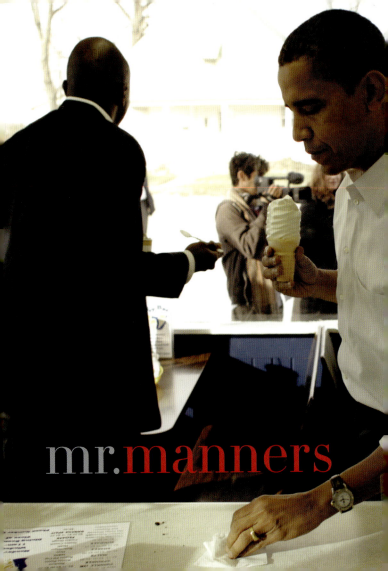

Mr. Manners: Lessons from Obama on Civility
copyright © 2010 by The Emily Post Institute, Inc.
All rights reserved. Printed in China.
No part of this book may be used or reproduced
in any manner whatsoever without written
permission except in the case of reprints in the
context of reviews. For information, write Andrews
McMeel Publishing, LLC, an Andrews McMeel
Universal company, 1130 Walnut Street, Kansas
City, Missouri 64106.

10 11 12 13 14 SDB 10 9 8 7 6 5 4 3 2 1

ISBN-13: 978-0-7407-9336-3
ISBN-10: 0-7407-9336-5

Library of Congress Control Number: 2009938769

www.andrewsmcmeel.com

Attention: Schools and Businesses
Andrews McMeel books are available
at quantity discounts with bulk purchase
for educational, business, or sales
promotional use. For information,
please write to:
   Special Sales Department
   Andrews McMeel Publishing, LLC
   1130 Walnut Street
   Kansas City, Missouri 64106.

**Produced by Smallwood & Stewart, Inc.,
New York City**

introduction

President Obama has made civility and good manners a hallmark of his career and his personal life. His actions speak loudly; there are thousands of examples, some of the best of which are captured in the images in these pages. He has also lent his words to the matter, speaking frequently of the importance of civility: "I am the eternal optimist. I think that, over time, people respond to civility…" Mr. Obama, from my line of work, I can agree: Yes, they certainly do.

Etiquette and manners matter as much today as they ever have. We see this in ubiquitous etiquette signs at the gym and the movies, boxes of thank-you note cards in stationery stores, and the media frenzies when a celebrity slips up. We also hear it in every "please" or "thank-you" that peppers our daily lives and see it in the many kind acts that we often call "paying it forward."

I'm sometimes asked how manners come to be. In most cases, they reflect how we, as a society, want to experience our surroundings and each other. When cell phones first came on the scene, for example, there was anarchy—people used them everywhere, for every reason, and at every volume. Now, most restaurants don't even need signs; the desire to have them off when they might bother others has become virtually unspoken.

Manners do change over time. Our society advances, so how we interact as part of it changes, too. We see this in the disappearance of chaperones and calling cards, and in new standards for new technology, such as cell phones and social networks. But there are some aspects of etiquette that are tried and true, gold standards unchanged no matter the times, no matter the culture. These essential principles of how we treat one another are consideration, respect, and honesty. There are certainly others, such as kindness, compassion, and graciousness, but these fundamental three are at the very core of everything else. They are the standard to look to when you are unsure of how to act. Satisfy these in your dealings with others and you're sure to come up with the right course of action every time.

President Obama offers many examples of how to do this. This book can't possibly capture them all, but I hope it gives you inspiration to apply to your own life. I hope it spurs awareness of all the places, small and large, where you can find opportunities to use manners to brighten your day, and others' as well.

—ANNA POST

personal lessons

Emily Post once said, "Any time two people come together and their actions affect one another, you have etiquette." This takes manners into every encounter we have, everywhere we go. After all, it's hard to be either rude or polite in a room by yourself; it takes two people.

Our personal manners are about how we put our fundamental values into the small gestures we make every day. These are common courtesies, and they do matter. Smile and say "hello" to those you live or work with in the morning. Offer a "please" or "thank you" to turn a demand into a request. It's important to show respect for ourselves, too, by accepting others' thanks with a simple "you're welcome." Hold doors or say "excuse me" if you bump someone to show you are aware and considerate of those around you, whether you know them or not.

These gestures are most sincere when they are natural. Make them a part of your daily life, whether you are with your best friend or a checkout clerk, your co-worker or your client, your family or a waiter. Courtesy never goes out of style, and you will stand out, just as President Obama does.

LEARN FROM THE GAME OF LIFE

Playing sports and other games can provide great models for life. Being a team player, respecting the customs of the setting you are in, embracing good fortune, and dealing with bad breaks graciously are skills that will sustain us in all kinds of situations.

---

lessons on the playing field and off

BE PREPARED

---

the power of practice

Although few of us will ever rehearse for an inauguration, as President Obama is here, no one wants to be caught unprepared. Being prepared before you enter a new situation, large or small, enables you to put others at ease while presenting yourself most graciously.

ACCEPT ADVICE GRACEFULLY

everyone has room
for improvement

Being open to advice, even
if it's over a minor detail,
is a sign of confidence and
self-assurance.

PUT YOUR BEST FOOT FORWARD

keep up appearances

Manners maketh the man, but a well-cut suit and a great tie go a long way, too. Although not every occasion calls for formal attire, dressing appropriately to the situation and with care will impress others and get you taken seriously.

BE PUNCTUAL

if you're not early, you're late

Etiquette is about respect, and one of the best ways to show our respect is to be on time. It's a simple habit that has profound consequences. Otherwise, our first words are, "I'm sorry"— not the message anyone wants to begin with.

ACT CONSIDERATELY

the impact of small gestures

Being thoughtful of others is the essence of civility. On an everyday level, it's demonstrated by small gestures, from cleaning up after yourself to holding the door for someone.

FIND A ROLE MODEL

benefit from their experience

Looking up to someone is not just for kids. Having a role model is a way to anchor your ideals and guide your actions. Parent, neighbor, or former president, it's smart to keep good company.

private lessons

In our private lives, our families and friends see us "behind the scenes." Although manners are important for big occasions, they matter just as much for the day-to-day events, as well. How we act in public sends a message about who we are to those who don't know us. How we act in private, with those who do know us, demonstrates our respect for family and friends.

Children soak up our examples, and setting good ones will give them an important base to grow from. Have dinner as a family as often as possible. Not only is it a chance to enjoy one another's company, it's a time to both teach children the manners you want them to have and to weed out any inappropriate behavior or language ("bus talk," my mom called it).

Most importantly, your private life is the time to relax and pursue what interests you. Use common courtesies and consideration for those around you to make that time all the more enjoyable.

SET AN EXAMPLE

model behavior

The best way to teach children is to lead by example. Practicing good manners at home makes it easy to expect good manners from kids when in public, too.

GIVE YOUR ATTENTION

the art of listening

Good communicators are good listeners, and good listeners give all their attention to the person they are with. Whether with children or adults, communication is often about acknowledging that you heard and understood the other person.

PRACTICE THOUGHTFULNESS

it's not just the thought that counts

No matter how busy or distracted you are, it's important to keep your priorities straight. Giving flowers is still one of the most classic ways to show love and affection. Taking the time to express your appreciation or love for those nearest to you is an essential part of nurturing good relationships.

ACT COURTEOUSLY

the romance of classic manners

Chivalry may sound like an old-fashioned word, but its values still resonate today. There's nothing so romantic as a gentleman giving his seat to a lady, or offering his jacket when she's chilly.

THE WHITE HOUSE

Dear Tephanie —
Thanks for your inspiring letter. I will do everything that I can to make sure young people like you get the very best education possible!

Barack Obama

sometimes the medium truly is the message

COMMUNICATE WELL

E-mail may be faster, but it doesn't have the impact of a letter written by hand. No matter how brief the message, a handwritten note shows how much you value someone and is a welcome surprise in a mailbox full of bills and catalogs.

public lessons

Although few of us will ever be in the public eye quite the way President Obama is, we all have big events, both personal and professional, when it's our turn to shine. By making etiquette part of our everyday lives, we don't need to think about it when the spotlight is on us. Our focus can stay where we want it—on the big presentation, speech, or event.

How we act in public says a lot about our self-awareness, something every successful person has. Staying focused on our goals while remaining attentive to and considerate of those around us is what having self-awareness is all about. Whether it's staying off our cell phones at the checkout counter or holding a door for someone who needs help, we say we are aware not only of ourselves but of those around us and how we might be affecting them. We're also saying that we want every interaction to be positive.

Manners give us confidence, something rather handy when all eyes are on us. People like working or spending time with people who are confident, and it feels good to walk into any situation and know that you understand what's expected of you and how to act. When you are confident of your manners, they simply become a part of you. In turn, your focus is on what you're there to do: to enjoy the benefit of building good relationships with others.

At the Table

main-street diner or high-state dinner, the same basic rules apply

A credit to the woman who raised him, the president uses his napkin to gently wipe his mouth. The most basic table manners call for using utensils (work from the outside in), not speaking with your mouth full, and thanking your host at the end of the meal. When in doubt, watch someone who looks like they know what they're doing and follow their lead.

WELCOME OTHERS

make the right first impression

Politicians learn early that good eye contact when shaking hands is a sign of recognition, welcome, and, most importantly, confidence. A firm handshake when meeting someone for the first time puts them at ease and begins everything on the right note.

Observe Formalities

---

because we all know
people who need
to be treated royally

Proper situations require
proper introductions: The
president introduces Mrs.
Obama to the Prince of Wales
and his wife, Camilla, Duchess
of Cornwall. The trick to
getting introductions right is
to speak to the more honored
person first: "Your Highness,
may I introduce my wife,
Michelle Obama, to you."

BE ATTENTIVE

when in doubt, simply ask

Men don't hold chairs for women because they're helpless; they do it as a sign of respect and to be attentive. Secretary Clinton can clearly manage on her own, but the gesture is a courteous one. If you're in doubt nowadays about whether or not to hold a woman's chair, simply ask, "May I hold your chair?" Her "Thanks" or "No, thanks" will let you know.

BE A GOOD HOST

leave a lasting impression

Always a good host, President Obama sees off his guest, King Abdullah of Jordan, by accompanying him all the way to the car. A polite welcome makes a good first impression, and a gracious good-bye leaves a lasting one.

BE
A GOOD
GUEST

when in rome

Travel is all about experiencing other cultures and being a good ambassador for your own. Showing respect for others' traditions can require a small step to take a bigger step toward building a good dialogue, such as when President Obama visited a mosque in Turkey.

RESPECT OTHERS

choose how to use technology

Cell phones, BlackBerrys, and other digital devices are just tools—it's how we choose to use them that make them welcome or offensive. Turn digital devices off for meetings—or better yet, leave them outside. Checking your e-mail in meetings or during a conversation is not just rude to everyone, it's distracting and rarely necessary, even in the White House.

HONOR DIGNITY

lend a helping hand

Escorting someone who needs assistance requires tact: Don't just take their arm, ask if they would like to take yours. Then match your pace to theirs, as President Obama does here with former first lady Nancy Reagan.

Keep It Simple

sometimes less is more

A toast or speech is often the pivotal
moment of an important event.
A good toast requires sincerity,
a little humor, and above all, brevity.
If you are the one being honored,
accept the toast as you would any
other compliment—with a smile
and a nod of the head. And,
remember, you don't drink when
someone toasts you.

what can you bring to the table?

BE A TEAM PLAYER

Leaders don't distinguish themselves by standing apart, they get in the action. Good manners are the same way: It's never about being aloof, it's about participating.

GIVE BACK

actions speak louder than words

Even a president can find time to
give back to the community.
Etiquette is about how your actions
affect others, and it doesn't get any
better than reaching out to help
your neighbors.

photo credits

Cover: AP; 2–3 Callie Shell, Aurora Photos; 5 Pete Souza/MAI/Landov; 13 Corbis; 14 Callie Shell, Aurora Photos; 16 Callie Shell, Aurora Photos; 19 Callie Shell, Aurora Photos; 20–21 Getty; 22–23 Callie Shell, Aurora Photos; 24 Corbis; 28–29 Callie Shell, Aurora Photos; 30–31 Getty; 32 AP; 35 Callie Shell, Aurora Photos; 36 Callie Shell, Aurora Photos; 41 Getty; 43 Rodionov Vladimir/ITARR-TASS/Landov; 45 AP; 46–47 AP; 48 AP; 50–51 Callie Shell, Aurora Photos; 52 Callie Shell, Aurora Photos; 55 Getty; 57 Getty; 58 Atlas; 60 Corbis; 62–63 Corbis.

Many thanks to Michelle Molloy for photo research.